The Animal Of Pride

Joshua Rhoades

Published by Joshua Paul Rhoades, 2024.

THE ANIMAL OF PRIDE

First edition. October 19, 2024.

ISBN: 979-8227752413

Written by Joshua Rhoades.

Also by Joshua Rhoades

Courage Under Fire: David's Stand On The Battlefield
Jonah's Journey: Voices Of Redemption And Lessons In Obedience
The Furnace Of Faith: 12 Principles From The Heat Of Faith
Whispers of Hope: Inspiring Stories of Men's Prayers In Scripture
Frontier Legends: The Oregon Dream
Elijah: A Beacon Of Boldness
HOOK, LINE & SAVIOUR - Faith Reflections from Fishing
Driven By Faith: Motor Racing Inspired Christian Life
30 Day Devotional - Bold and Strong- Coffee Devotions for a Courageous
Christian Walk
Authentic Christianity: The Heart of Old Time Religion
Consider The Ant - God's Tiny Preachers
Flee Fornication: The Plea For Purity
Renewed Hope- How to Find Encouragement in God
Sounding The Call - The Voice of Conviction
The Altar - Where Heaven Meets Earth
The Bible's Battlefields- Timeless Lessons from Ancient Wars
The Sacred Art of Silence - How Silence Speaks in Scripture
Under Fire- The Sanctity of the Traditional Biblical Home
Who Is on the Lord's Side? A Call to Righteousness
What Is Truth? - From Skepticism to Submission
First and Goal- Faith and Football Fundamentals
From Dugout to Devotion- Spiritual Lessons from Baseball
Par for the Course- Faith and Fairways
The Believer's Pace- Tools for Running Life's Marathon
The Immutable Fortress- Security in God's Unchanging Nature
Biblical Bravery
Deer Stands and Devotions: A Hunter's Walk with God

Jesus Knows- Our Hearts, Our Responsibility
Restoration - Setting The Bone
Spiritual 911- God's Word for Life's Emergency's
The Freedom of Forgiveness
The Jezebel Effect - Ancient Manipulations Modern Lessons
The Shout That Stopped The Saviour
The Time Machine Chronicles: Old Testament Characters
Anchored In Truth Exploring The Depths of Psalm 119
Biblical Counsel on Anger
Proverbs' Portraits The Men God Mentions
Stumbling in the Dark - The Dangers of Alcohol
Guarding the Wicket Protecting Your Faith and Game
The Champion's Faith - Wrestling and Achieving Spiritual Victory
Scriptural Commands for Modern Times Living God's Word Today Volume 1
Scriptural Commands for Modern Times Living God's Word Today Volume 2
Scriptural Commands for Modern Times Living God's Word TodayVolume3
The Greatest Gift
A Christmas Journey of Faith
Daughter Of The King: Embracing Your Identity In Christ
Determination and Dedication Building Strong Faith As A Young Man
Walking Through Walls God's Power to Part the Storms of Life
David's Song Of Deliverance Praising God Through Every Storm
From Weakness to Warrior: Gideon's Transformation
Why Did Jesus Weep?
Living For God The Call To Be A Living Sacrifice
My Mind Is In A Fog What Do I Do?
Turning The Page Written By Grace
The Calling and Greatness of John the Baptist
For Such a Time Esther's Courageous Stand
From Brokenness To Beauty Written By The Pen of Grace
The Ultimate Guide to Massive Action- From Plans to Reality
A Heart Of Conviction
Serving In The Shadows
Repentance Revealed The Road Back To God
The Chief Sinner Meets The Chief Saviour Reflections On I Timothy 1:15

Answer The Call - 31 Days of Biblical Action
The Birthmark of the Believer
Reflections on Calvary's Cross
The Kingdom Builder Paul's Bold Proclamation of Christ
The Animal Of Pride

Dedication

This book is dedicated to you, the reader, with a heart full of hope and encouragement as you journey through the pages of "The Animal of Pride." I know that the battle with pride is not an easy one; it's something we all face in one way or another, often without realizing how deeply it affects our hearts, our relationships, and our connection with God. It can sneak up on us when we feel strong or confident, making us believe we are in control, that we don't need anyone's help, or that we are somehow better than others. But my hope for you, as you read this book, is that you will find comfort in knowing that you are not alone in this struggle. We all wrestle with pride, and we all have moments when it gets the better of us. Yet, in those moments, there is also an incredible opportunity for growth, for healing, and for drawing closer to God. I dedicate this book to you because I believe in the power of humility, in the strength that comes not from exalting ourselves, but from surrendering to God's will, and in the peace that comes from letting go of the need to be in control. As you reflect on the ways pride has crept into your life—whether in big ways or small—may you also find the courage to confront it, to name it for what it is, and to ask God to help you overcome it. This is not a journey you have to walk alone. With God's grace, pride can be tamed, and you can experience the freedom that comes from living a life of humility, where your heart is open to love, to service, and to the blessings God has for you. This book is also dedicated to your desire for deeper relationships—both with the people around you and with God. Pride has a way of putting walls between us and those we love, making it harder to connect, to forgive, and to truly see one another. But I believe that by recognizing pride in our own hearts, by humbling ourselves and choosing to listen, to forgive, and to serve, we can break down those walls and build relationships that are stronger, more compassionate, and more filled with grace. As you turn each page, may you feel inspired to live in a way that reflects Christ's humility and love, knowing that humility is not about thinking less of yourself, but about thinking of yourself less and making room for God to work in your life. I dedicate this book to the moments when you feel overwhelmed by pride, when it feels like it has taken hold of your heart and you're not sure how to break free. I want you to know that there is always hope. God is with you in this struggle, and He is ready to help you overcome pride if you will invite Him into your heart. He doesn't expect perfection, and He doesn't condemn you for the times you've stumbled. Instead, He offers grace, mercy, and the strength to get back up and try again. This book is a reminder that God's love for you is not based on your accomplishments, your status, or how others see you. His love is unconditional, and His grace is sufficient for every moment of weakness. I hope you will take comfort in that truth as you work to tame the animal of pride in your life. Lastly, I dedicate this book to your journey of faith. As you seek to grow closer to God, to walk in humility, and to live a life that honors Him, may this book serve as a guide and an encouragement. Pride will always be something we must guard against, but with God's help, it doesn't have to control us. As you continue on your journey, may you find strength in God's Word, peace in His presence, and joy in knowing that He is shaping you into the person He created you to be. Thank you for opening your heart to this message, and may God bless you as you take the next steps on your journey of faith. This book is for you.

Introduction

Pride is a powerful force, like a wild animal lurking in the shadows, waiting to strike when we least expect it. In "The Animal of Pride," we explore how pride behaves, often like the most dangerous creatures in the wild. Pride can creep into our hearts without warning, and before we know it, it has taken control, shaping our thoughts, actions, and relationships in ways that we might not even notice. It is like a lion stalking its prey, silently moving in until it is too late to escape. It can roar like a beast, making us boastful and eager for attention, or it can slither in quietly like a snake, hiding itself behind false humility and good intentions. Pride digs deep into our hearts like a mole, burrowing beneath the surface until it emerges as stubbornness, arrogance, or selfishness. It multiplies like a pack of wolves, spreading from one small thought of superiority into a whole host of sinful behaviors—greed, envy, anger, and bitterness—all working together to pull us further away from God and from the people we love. This book is an honest exploration of how pride shows up in our lives, often without us realizing it, and how it can quickly spiral out of control. Just like a horse in battle, pride charges ahead recklessly, not caring who it hurts along the way, and its sting is sharp, like the tail of a scorpion, causing pain to ourselves and those around us. But pride doesn't just affect our relationships with others; it also damages our relationship with God. It blinds us to the truth, making us think we don't need Him, that we can handle life on our own. Pride tells us that we are strong enough, smart enough, and good enough to succeed without help, but this is a lie. The truth is, pride separates us from God's grace and keeps us from experiencing the peace, love, and joy that He wants to give us. In this book, we will take a close look at the many ways pride acts like an animal—fierce, unpredictable, and often destructive—and how it can tear apart our lives if we let it. But there is hope. Just as wild animals can be tamed, pride can be defeated. By recognizing it for what it is, by humbling ourselves before God, and by allowing His love to transform us, we can break free from the hold pride has on us. This journey isn't easy, but it's worth it. "The Animal of Pride" will challenge you to see yourself in a new light, to confront the areas of your life where pride may be hiding, and to take steps toward a life of humility, grace, and peace. We'll explore how to recognize the warning signs of pride before it takes control, how to resist the temptation to put ourselves first, and how to seek God's guidance in all things. If you're ready to face the animal of pride head-on, then this book is for you. Together, we'll discover the strength that comes not from pride, but from humility, and the freedom that comes from surrendering our lives to the One who loves us most. Let's begin the journey of taming the animal of pride, and finding the true peace and fulfillment that only God can provide.

Chapter 1 - Pride Stalks Silently Like A Predator

Pride is like a predator that stalks silently, moving so carefully that we often don't see it coming. Just as a lion creeps through the tall grass, hidden from its prey, so too does pride creep into our hearts without us even noticing. It begins with a small thought or feeling, maybe the belief that we are better than someone else, or the desire to be recognized and praised. These feelings seem harmless at first, but pride is dangerous, and if left unchecked, it grows stronger, just like a lion getting closer to its prey, ready to pounce. The Bible warns us about this, especially in 1 Peter 5:8, which says, "Be sober, be vigilant; because your adversary the devil, as a roaring lion, walketh about, seeking whom he may devour." Here, the devil is compared to a roaring lion, but this also applies to pride. Pride, like the devil, is always looking for a way to enter our lives and take over our hearts. We must be vigilant, or careful, always on the lookout for pride trying to sneak in. It doesn't come loudly or boldly at first. It comes silently, making us believe that we are just confident or that we are doing well. But there's a fine line between confidence and pride, and once that line is crossed, pride takes control. When we think of a lion stalking its prey, we see how quiet and patient it is. It doesn't rush, but instead waits for the right moment to strike. Pride is the same. It waits until we are not paying attention, until we have let our guard down, and then it begins to take over our thoughts. It can start with something simple, like thinking we deserve more praise for something we've done. Maybe we believe we are smarter, stronger, or better than others, and we start to look down on them. This is the first sign that pride is beginning to take over. Like a predator, pride begins to circle around us, looking for more ways to attack. It might cause us to seek out compliments or to boast about ourselves. We might start comparing ourselves to others, always believing that we are better. This is how pride works. It feeds on our insecurities and our desire for approval. At first, we may not notice it, but soon, it becomes a habit. We constantly look for ways to make ourselves feel more important, and before we know it, pride has taken over our thoughts and actions. Just as a lion must be stopped before it can strike, we must stop pride before it grows too strong. The Bible tells us to "be sober," which means to be serious and aware of what is happening in our hearts. We must not allow pride to grow. Instead, we must be humble and remind ourselves that everything we have comes from God. The skills, talents, and abilities that we are proud of are gifts from Him, and we should use them to serve others, not to make ourselves look better. The verse also tells us to "be vigilant," meaning to be watchful. We should be aware of the moments when pride starts to creep in, and we must act quickly to stop it. Like a predator, pride waits for the perfect opportunity to take over, but we must not give it that chance. Pride often disguises itself as something good. It might make us think we are just being confident or standing up for ourselves. But there's a difference between healthy confidence and pride. Confidence is knowing that God has given us the ability to do something well, and we use that ability to glorify Him and help others. Pride, on the other hand, is when we believe we are better than others because of our abilities. This is where the danger lies. When pride takes over, we stop relying on God and start relying on ourselves. We forget that it is God who gives us strength, and instead, we believe that we are strong on our own. Just as a lion's prey is unaware of the danger until it is too late, we can be unaware of how pride is taking over our hearts until it has already caused harm. It can damage our relationships with others, making us boastful, selfish, and unkind. It can also damage our relationship with God because pride makes us believe that we don't need Him. We might not pray as much, thinking that we can handle everything on our own. We might not seek His guidance because we believe we know what is best. This is how pride separates us from God, just as a lion separates its prey from the safety of the herd. The devil, as a roaring lion, uses pride to devour us. He knows that pride is a powerful tool to lead us away from God. He wants us to be filled with pride because it makes us vulnerable to other sins, such as envy, greed, and anger. When pride takes root in our hearts, it opens the door for these other sins to enter. We begin to compare ourselves to others, becoming envious of what they have. We become greedy, wanting more for ourselves. We become angry when things don't go our way, believing that we deserve better. This is how pride leads to destruction. It starts small but grows quickly, just like a lion stalking its prey. The lion does not attack right away but waits for the perfect moment when the prey is weak or distracted. Pride does the same. It waits until we are not paying attention, until we are feeling confident and secure, and then it strikes. By the time we realize what has happened, pride has already done its damage. It has separated us from God and caused harm to our relationships with others. This is why we must be sober and vigilant, always on guard against the silent predator of pride. We must recognize the warning signs and act quickly to humble ourselves before God. The Bible tells us in Proverbs 16:18 that "Pride goeth before destruction, and an haughty spirit before a fall." Just as a lion's prey is destroyed once it is caught, we too will face destruction if we allow pride to take over our hearts. But there is hope. Just as a lion can be stopped before it attacks, pride can be stopped before it causes harm. We must turn to God in humility, recognizing that all we have comes from Him. We must remind ourselves that we are not better than others, and that our worth comes from being children of God, not from our achievements or abilities. By doing this, we can stop pride in its tracks and prevent it from leading us to destruction. The Bible also tells us in James 4:6 that "But he giveth more grace. Wherefore he saith, God resisteth the proud, but giveth grace unto the humble." When we humble ourselves before God, He gives us the strength and grace to overcome pride. We must be watchful, always on guard, because pride is a silent predator, waiting to attack when we least expect it. Like a lion stalking its prey, pride is patient and cunning, but with God's help, we can resist it and live in humility, relying on Him for all things.

Chapter 2 - Pride Devours Like A Lion

Pride is like a lion that devours everything in its path. At first, it may seem small and harmless, but once pride takes root in a person's heart, it begins to consume them, just like a lion devouring its prey. The Bible warns us in Proverbs 16:18, "Pride goeth before destruction, and an haughty spirit before a fall." This means that when pride takes over, it leads to our downfall, leaving us blind to our own mistakes and weaknesses. Pride is sneaky; it doesn't come all at once. It starts with little things like wanting praise for something we did or thinking we're better than someone else. These thoughts seem innocent, but they grow quickly, like a lion getting ready to pounce on its prey. Before we know it, pride has taken over, and we can't see how it's controlling us. When pride devours a person, they stop seeing their own faults. They become blind to their weaknesses, thinking that they are always right and everyone else is wrong. This is the danger of pride. It makes us think we are perfect, even when we are not. It makes us believe that we don't need to change, that we don't need help, and that we are better than those around us. Just like a lion devouring its prey, pride devours our ability to see clearly. It eats away at our humility and replaces it with arrogance and a haughty spirit. We start to think that we are more important than we really are, and we stop listening to others. Pride makes us think that we are always right and that we don't need anyone else's advice or guidance. This is why pride leads to destruction, as Proverbs 16:18 says. When pride consumes us, it leads to a fall. Just like a lion that devours its prey, leaving nothing behind, pride leaves us empty and broken. It may feel good at first to be proud, but eventually, it destroys us from the inside out. Pride makes us blind to the truth, and when we can't see the truth, we make bad decisions. We hurt others without realizing it, and we damage our relationships. We stop relying on God and start relying on ourselves, thinking that we can do everything on our own. But pride is deceptive, and it always leads to a fall. When we think we are standing strong, pride is actually setting us up for failure. It's like a lion waiting for the perfect moment to strike. It waits until we are not paying attention, and then it devours us. The Bible is clear that pride is dangerous. It not only leads to destruction, but it also separates us from God. When we are consumed by pride, we don't think we need God. We believe that we are in control of our own lives, and we stop seeking God's guidance. This is the biggest danger of pride. It pulls us away from God, making us think that we don't need Him. But the truth is, we need God more than anything. Without Him, we are like sheep lost in the wilderness, vulnerable to the attacks of the lion. Pride makes us think we are strong, but in reality, it makes us weak. It blinds us to our need for God, and without Him, we are powerless. Just as a lion devours its prey, pride devours our relationship with God. It separates us from His love and guidance, leaving us alone and vulnerable. Pride not only affects our relationship with God, but it also affects our relationships with others. When we are consumed by pride, we stop caring about the feelings and needs of those around us. We become selfish and arrogant, thinking only of ourselves. Pride makes us think that we are better than others, and this leads to conflict and division. We start to look down on others, thinking that we are more important or more valuable than they are. This is another way that pride leads to destruction. It destroys our relationships and causes division among friends, family, and even in the church. Pride devours the love and unity that God wants us to have with one another. It replaces kindness and compassion with arrogance and selfishness. When we are consumed by pride, we stop seeing others as equals, and we start treating them as less than ourselves. This is not what God wants for us. He calls us to love one another and to put others before ourselves. But pride makes this impossible. It devours our ability to love and serve others, leaving us isolated and alone. Just as a lion devours its prey, leaving nothing behind, pride leaves us empty and alone. It takes away our joy, our peace, and our ability to connect with others. When we are consumed by pride, we are constantly striving to prove ourselves, to be better than others, and to receive praise and recognition. But this is a never-ending cycle. No matter how much praise we receive, it is never enough. Pride is never satisfied. It always wants more. And in the end, it leaves us feeling empty and unfulfilled. The Bible warns us that pride leads to destruction because it takes us away from the things that truly matter. It makes us focus on ourselves instead of on God and on loving others. It makes us believe that we are more important than we really are, and this leads to our downfall. Just as a lion devours its prey, pride devours our ability to see the truth. It blinds us to our own faults and weaknesses, making us think that we are invincible. But the truth is, we are not. We are all human, and we all have weaknesses and faults. Pride makes us forget this, and when we forget this, we are setting ourselves up for failure. The Bible tells us that "Pride goeth before destruction, and an haughty spirit before a fall." This means that when we allow pride to take over, we are heading for a fall. It may not happen right away, but eventually, pride will lead to our downfall. Just as a lion waits patiently for the right moment to strike, pride waits for the right moment to devour us. It waits until we are feeling confident and secure, and then it strikes, leaving us blind to the truth and vulnerable to destruction. But there is hope. Just as we can protect ourselves from a lion by being vigilant and aware of its presence, we can protect ourselves from pride by being humble and aware of its dangers. The Bible tells us that God gives grace to the humble, but He resists the proud. When we humble ourselves before God, we are protected from the devouring power of pride. We recognize that we are not better than others, and we acknowledge our need for God's guidance and help. This humility is what keeps pride from devouring us. It allows us to see our faults and weaknesses, and it keeps us dependent on God's strength instead of our own. In the end, pride is like a lion that devours everything in its path. It consumes our ability to see the truth, it destroys our relationships, and it separates us from God. But when we humble ourselves and recognize our need for God, we are protected from the destructive power of pride. Just as a lion can be stopped before it devours its prey, pride can be stopped before it leads to our destruction. We must be vigilant, always on guard against the dangers of pride, and we must rely on God's strength to keep us humble and free from its devouring power. Pride is a powerful force, but with God's help, we can overcome it and live in humility, recognizing that everything we have comes from Him, and that without Him, we are nothing. Pride may try to devour us like a lion, but with God's grace, we can stand strong and resist its power, living lives that honor Him and reflect His love and humility to the world.

Chapter 3 - Pride Roars Like A Lion

Pride roars like a lion, making itself known to everyone around. It wants attention, it wants recognition, and it craves admiration from others. Pride is not content to stay quiet or humble; instead, it seeks the spotlight, making sure everyone knows how great, powerful, or important it is. When pride roars, it sounds like boasting, and the louder the roar, the more it tries to convince the world that it is the greatest. But in reality, pride's loud roar is just a way to cover up insecurity and weakness, because deep down, pride is afraid of being seen as less than perfect. The Bible warns us about this kind of boasting in James 4:16, which says, "But now ye rejoice in your boastings: all such rejoicing is evil." This verse makes it clear that when we take pride in our own achievements and boast about them, we are stepping into dangerous territory. Prideful boasting is not only unwise, but it is also evil, because it shifts our focus away from God and onto ourselves. Just like a lion's roar is a display of power, pride's boastful words are meant to show off strength and superiority. But while a lion roars to defend its territory or intimidate its rivals, pride roars to make sure everyone sees how important we think we are. It's not enough for pride to be good at something; it has to make sure that everyone else knows it too. Pride wants to be admired, praised, and envied. It seeks validation from others, and the louder it roars, the more it tries to drown out any feelings of inadequacy or failure. But the Bible tells us that all such boasting is wrong because it comes from a heart that is focused on self rather than on God. Prideful boasting is a way of saying, "Look at me, I did this on my own, I don't need anyone else's help." But the truth is, everything we have and everything we achieve comes from God. Without Him, we are nothing, and without His blessings, we could not accomplish anything of value. When pride roars, it forgets this truth. It forgets that all glory belongs to God and not to ourselves. The problem with pride is that it makes us think we are better than others. It causes us to look down on people who we think are less successful, less talented, or less important. Pride tells us that we deserve the credit for our successes and that we are superior to those who don't measure up. This is why pride is so dangerous—it separates us from others and from God. Instead of giving thanks to God for our blessings, we boast about them as if we earned them on our own. Instead of seeing others as equals, pride makes us see them as competitors, people we need to outshine or outdo. Pride thrives on comparison. It roars the loudest when it believes it has won, when it thinks it has proven itself better than everyone else. But this kind of boasting leads to destruction. Proverbs 16:18 warns us, "Pride goeth before destruction, and an haughty spirit before a fall." Just as a lion's roar can signal danger, pride's boastful roars signal that a fall is coming. When we allow pride to take over, we become blind to our own weaknesses, and we set ourselves up for failure. The more we boast, the more we rely on our own strength and forget that we need God's help. And when we stop relying on God, we become vulnerable to failure, just like a roaring lion that is too focused on showing off its strength and not paying attention to the dangers around it. Pride's roar can also damage our relationships with others. When we boast about our achievements, we push people away. No one likes to be around someone who is constantly bragging about how great they are. Prideful boasting creates distance between us and others because it makes them feel inferior or unimportant. Instead of building connections with others through kindness, humility, and empathy, pride's loud roar creates walls of arrogance and self-centeredness. It's hard to build meaningful relationships when all we do is talk about ourselves and how much better we are than everyone else. Pride also makes it difficult for us to accept help or advice from others. When we are full of pride, we think we know it all. We don't listen to other people's suggestions or wisdom because we believe we have all the answers. But the Bible teaches us that humility is the path to wisdom. Proverbs 11:2 says, "When pride cometh, then cometh shame: but with the lowly is wisdom." True wisdom comes from recognizing that we don't have all the answers and that we need God's guidance and the support of others. Pride's roaring, however, drowns out the voice of wisdom. It tells us that we are fine on our own, that we don't need anyone else's input, and that we can handle everything ourselves. This is why pride leads to destruction. It isolates us from the people who care about us, and it blinds us to our own limitations. Another problem with pride's roar is that it keeps us from seeing our need for repentance. When we are consumed with pride, we don't think we've done anything wrong. We become blind to our sins and faults because pride tells us that we are always in the right. This is why James 4:16 calls rejoicing in our boastings evil. Prideful boasting is a form of self-righteousness, a way of declaring that we don't need forgiveness because we believe we've done everything perfectly. But the Bible teaches us that none of us are perfect, and all of us need God's grace and mercy. Romans 3:23 reminds us, "For all have sinned, and come short of the glory of God." Pride tries to hide this truth from us. It tries to convince us that we don't need God's forgiveness because we are good enough on our own. But this is a dangerous lie. The louder pride roars, the more it blocks out the truth of our need for repentance and God's grace. Pride's roar also keeps us from growing in our faith. When we are full of pride, we think we've already arrived, that we've already learned everything there is to know. But the Christian life is a journey of continuous growth and learning. We are always in need of God's wisdom and guidance, and we should always be seeking to grow closer to Him. Pride, however, tells us that we don't need to keep growing, that we've already reached the top. This kind of thinking is dangerous because it keeps us stagnant in our faith. We stop seeking God's wisdom, we stop reading His Word, and we stop praying for His guidance because pride convinces us that we've already got everything figured out. But the Bible tells us that we should always be growing in our faith. 2 Peter 3:18 says, "But grow in grace, and in the knowledge of our Lord and Saviour Jesus Christ. To him be glory both now and for ever. Amen." Pride's roar, however, tries to stop this growth by convincing us that we've already learned enough. The antidote to pride's roar is humility. Instead of boasting about our own achievements, we should give glory to God for everything we have. Instead of seeking attention and praise for ourselves, we should seek to honor God with our words and actions. Humility reminds us that we are not the center of the universe, that we are not better than others, and that we are completely dependent on God for everything. When we embrace humility, we silence pride's roar. We stop seeking to boast about ourselves, and instead, we focus on serving others and glorifying God. The Bible teaches us that humility leads to honor. Proverbs 22:4 says, "By humility and the fear of the Lord are riches, and honour, and life." When we humble ourselves before God, He lifts us up in due time. Instead of trying to roar like a lion to make ourselves feel important, we should trust that God will exalt us in His perfect timing. In the end, pride's roar may be loud, but it is empty. It promises greatness, but it delivers destruction. It makes us think we are invincible, but it sets us up for a fall. It tells us we don't need God or others, but it leaves us alone and vulnerable. Pride's roar is a deceptive noise that tries to drown out the truth of our need for God's grace and the importance of humility. The louder pride roars, the more we should turn to God in humility, seeking His wisdom, guidance, and grace. Just as a lion's roar can be a warning of danger, pride's roar should remind us of the dangers of boasting and self-centeredness. Instead of rejoicing in our boastings, we should rejoice in the Lord, who gives us everything we have and who is the source of all true wisdom and strength. Pride may roar like a lion, but with God's help, we can silence that roar and walk in humility, living lives that honor Him and reflect His love to the world around us.

Chapter 4 - Pride Puffs Up Like A Peacock

Pride puffs up like a peacock, spreading its feathers wide, showing off to the world, making itself look larger and more important than it really is. Just like a peacock flaunting its colorful display, pride has a way of making a person feel bigger, better, and more significant than they actually are. But just as a peacock's feathers are a show of appearance rather than strength, pride is often based on false perceptions. It builds itself on the illusion of self-importance and creates a picture that might look impressive on the outside but is hollow on the inside. The Bible warns us about the danger of being puffed up with pride in 1 Corinthians 8:1, which says, "Now as touching things offered unto idols, we know that we all have knowledge. Knowledge puffeth up, but charity edifieth." This verse reminds us that while pride inflates our sense of self, it doesn't build anything real or lasting. True growth comes from love and humility, not from boasting or showing off. Pride, like the peacock's feathers, is often shallow. It draws attention, but it doesn't accomplish much beyond that. When someone is puffed up with pride, they are focused on making themselves look good, on receiving praise and admiration from others. They want to be noticed, admired, and envied. But all of this is based on external appearances, not on what really matters in the heart. The problem with pride is that it distorts reality. It makes us think we are more important than we are, just like a peacock's feathers make it look larger than it really is. When we are filled with pride, we start to believe that we are better than others. We look down on people who we think aren't as smart, talented, or successful as we are. Pride puffs us up, making us feel superior, but this feeling of superiority is an illusion. It's not based on truth, and it doesn't reflect the way God sees us or the way we should see ourselves. The Bible teaches us that God values humility, not pride. Proverbs 29:23 says, "A man's pride shall bring him low: but honour shall uphold the humble in spirit." This verse shows the contrast between pride and humility. While pride might lift us up in our own eyes and in the eyes of others for a moment, it ultimately brings us down. Like a peacock's feathers that can only stay open for a short time before falling back down, pride's inflated sense of self cannot last. It's temporary, and eventually, it will lead to a fall. Humility, on the other hand, leads to honor because it is based on a true understanding of ourselves and our need for God. When pride puffs us up, we lose sight of the truth. We forget that everything we have—our abilities, our talents, our achievements—comes from God. Instead of giving Him the glory, we start to take credit for everything ourselves. Pride whispers in our ear, telling us that we don't need anyone else, that we've made it on our own, and that we deserve all the praise. But this is a dangerous lie. The Bible tells us in James 4:6, "But he giveth more grace. Wherefore he saith, God resisteth the proud, but giveth grace unto the humble." When we are puffed up with pride, we are actually setting ourselves against God because we are rejecting the truth that we are dependent on Him for everything. Pride makes us believe that we are self-sufficient, but the reality is that we need God's grace every day. Just like a peacock cannot make its feathers any more beautiful by its own power, we cannot make ourselves truly great without God's help. Pride puffs up, but it doesn't produce anything of real value. It's all for show, like the peacock's feathers that may catch attention but don't serve any real purpose beyond that. True greatness doesn't come from being puffed up with pride; it comes from humility and love. That's why 1 Corinthians 8:1 contrasts pride with charity, or love. While pride puffs up, charity edifies—it builds up. Pride is focused on the self, on making oneself look good, but love is focused on others, on helping and serving them. Pride is about inflating our own importance, while love is about lifting others up. The Bible tells us that the greatest commandment is to love God and to love others (Matthew 22:37-39). When we are filled with pride, we cannot truly love others because pride turns our focus inward, making everything about us. But when we are humble, we can love others as God calls us to because humility allows us to see beyond ourselves. Pride puffs up, but love builds up. Another danger of pride is that it blinds us to our own faults. When we are puffed up with pride, we don't see our own mistakes or weaknesses. We are too busy admiring our own feathers, so to speak, to notice where we fall short. This is why pride is so destructive. It keeps us from growing and improving because it convinces us that we don't need to. Proverbs 16:18 warns us, "Pride goeth before destruction, and an haughty spirit before a fall." When we are puffed up with pride, we are setting ourselves up for failure because we are ignoring the areas where we need to change or seek help. Just like a peacock with its feathers spread wide is vulnerable to predators because it can't see the danger around it, a person puffed up with pride is vulnerable to failure because they can't see their own weaknesses. Pride makes us think we are invincible, but the truth is, we all have weaknesses and we all need God's help. Pride may puff us up for a while, but eventually, it leads to a fall because it separates us from the truth and from the people who could help us if we were humble enough to admit that we need help. Pride not only affects our relationship with God, but it also affects our relationships with others. When we are puffed up with pride, we push people away. No one wants to be around someone who is always showing off, always trying to make themselves look better than everyone else. Pride creates division because it sets us above others in our own minds. Instead of seeing people as equals, pride makes us see them as competitors, as people we need to outdo or impress. This is not how God calls us to live. Philippians 2:3 says, "Let nothing be done through strife or vainglory; but in lowliness of mind let each esteem other better than themselves." God calls us to humility, to put others before ourselves, but pride does the opposite. It makes everything about us, about how we can get ahead and how we can be admired. When we are puffed up with pride, we are not thinking about how we can serve others or how we can glorify God. We are only thinking about how we can make ourselves look good. Pride also keeps us from accepting correction or advice from others. When we are puffed up, we think we know everything. We don't listen to others because we believe we are always right. This is a dangerous attitude because it keeps us from learning and growing. Proverbs 11:2 says, "When pride cometh, then cometh shame: but with the lowly is wisdom." True wisdom comes from being humble, from being willing to listen to others and to admit that we don't have all the answers. But pride puffs us up and makes us think we don't need anyone else's advice or guidance. It isolates us, keeping us from the wisdom that could help us grow and succeed. Just as a peacock's feathers can only stay spread for so long before they have to come down, pride's inflated sense of self cannot last. Eventually, reality sets in, and we are forced to face the truth—that we are not as great or important as pride led us to believe. Pride may puff us up for a time, but it cannot sustain us. Only humility and dependence on God can lead to lasting success and fulfillment. The Bible is clear that God values humility over pride. Jesus Himself demonstrated this through His life. Philippians 2:5-8 says, "Let this mind be in you, which was also in Christ Jesus: Who, being in the form of God, thought it not robbery to be equal with God: But made himself of no reputation, and took upon him the form of a servant, and was made in the likeness of men: And being found in fashion as a man, he humbled himself, and became obedient unto death, even the death of the cross." Jesus, who had every reason to be proud, chose humility. He didn't puff Himself up or seek to be admired. Instead, He humbled Himself and served others, even to the point of dying on the cross for our sins. This is the example we are called to follow. Instead of being puffed up with pride, we are called to humble ourselves and serve others, just as Jesus did. Pride may promise glory, but it leads to destruction. Humility may seem less glamorous, but it leads to true honor and life. When we are puffed up with pride, we are like a peacock showing off its feathers, trying to impress others with our appearance. But God doesn't look at the outward appearance; He looks at the heart. 1 Samuel 16:7 states "But the Lord said unto Samuel, Look not on his countenance, or on the height of his stature; because I have refused him: for the Lord seeth not as man seeth; for man looketh on the outward appearance, but the Lord looketh on the heart." What matters to God is not how we look or how much we can boast about our achievements, but how we love and serve others. Pride puffs up, but it doesn't build up. It creates a false image of ourselves that can't last. But when we humble ourselves and focus on loving others, we build something real and lasting. We build relationships, we build character, and we build a life that honors God. Pride may puff us up for a moment, but humility is what truly lifts us up in God's eyes. Just like the peacock's feathers, pride's display is temporary, but the impact of a humble heart lasts forever.

Chapter 5 - Pride Is Stubborn Like A Mule

Pride is stubborn like a mule, digging in its heels and refusing to move, no matter how much it is prodded or corrected. Just like a mule that won't budge when it doesn't want to, pride makes a person unyielding and unwilling to admit when they are wrong. This kind of stubbornness is dangerous because it blocks growth, repentance, and the ability to learn from mistakes. Proverbs 29:1 warns us about the consequences of such pride, saying, "He, that being often reproved hardeneth his neck, shall suddenly be destroyed, and that without remedy." The imagery of hardening one's neck is a picture of someone who refuses to bend or listen to correction, much like a mule that stiffens its body and resists any effort to move it. Pride behaves the same way. When we are filled with pride, we don't want to admit our faults or acknowledge that we need to change. We become like that stubborn mule, convinced that we are right, even when we are clearly wrong, and this stubbornness leads to our downfall. The Bible teaches that God sends reproof, or correction, to guide us and help us stay on the right path, but pride makes us resist that correction. Instead of learning and growing, pride makes us dig in deeper, refusing to admit that we need to change or that we might not have all the answers. This is where the stubbornness of pride becomes most harmful. Just as a mule's refusal to move can keep it from reaching safety or finding food, pride's refusal to admit fault keeps us from growing spiritually, relationally, and personally. It keeps us stuck in the same place, unable to move forward because we refuse to acknowledge that we need help or that we've made a mistake.

Pride is like a stubborn mule in the way it makes a person unwilling to listen to advice or accept guidance. Even when people who care about us try to offer correction or help us see our errors, pride blocks our ears. We harden our hearts and refuse to hear what others are saying. This stubbornness can damage relationships, cause misunderstandings, and lead to isolation, because no one wants to constantly deal with someone who refuses to listen or change. Pride not only damages our relationships with others but also affects our relationship with God. Just as a mule refuses to follow its master's lead, pride causes us to resist God's direction in our lives. God may try to show us the right path or correct us when we stray, but pride makes us resist Him. We tell ourselves that we know better that we don't need to listen to His guidance, and that we can handle things on our own. This is a dangerous attitude because, as Proverbs 29:1 says, "He, that being often reproved hardeneth his neck, shall suddenly be destroyed, and that without remedy." In other words, pride leads to destruction because it prevents us from accepting the very correction that could save us. God, in His love and mercy, offers us guidance and correction, but pride makes us reject it. It makes us think we don't need God's help, that we can do everything on our own, and that admitting we are wrong would somehow make us weak or less important. But the truth is, admitting our faults and accepting correction is a sign of strength, not weakness. It takes humility and courage to recognize that we are not perfect and that we need God's help.

The stubbornness of pride can be compared to a mule's refusal to move, even when it's in its own best interest. Just as a mule might resist being led to water or food, pride makes us resist the very things that would benefit us. We might know deep down that we need to change, that we need to apologize, or that we need to take a different path, but pride keeps us from doing so. It tells us that changing would mean admitting defeat, and pride never wants to admit defeat. It wants to win at all costs, even if that means remaining stuck or heading down the wrong path. This is why pride is so destructive. It doesn't just affect our actions; it affects our mindset and keeps us trapped in a cycle of stubbornness and resistance. Pride blinds us to the truth and makes us unwilling to see things from any perspective other than our own. It tells us that we are always right, that we don't need to change, and that everyone else is wrong. This is the kind of stubbornness that Proverbs 29:1 is warning about. The person who is constantly corrected but refuses to listen is headed for destruction because they are shutting themselves off from the truth. They are closing their hearts to the wisdom that could save them.

Another way that pride is like a stubborn mule is in its resistance to repentance. Just as a mule refuses to move when it doesn't want to, pride keeps us from turning away from sin and seeking forgiveness. It tells us that we don't need to repent, that we haven't done anything wrong, or that admitting our sin would make us look weak or foolish. But the Bible teaches us that repentance is essential to our relationship with God. Proverbs 28:13 says, "He that covereth his sins shall not prosper: but whoso confesseth and forsaketh them shall have mercy." Pride, however, makes us want to cover up our sins rather than confess them. It makes us stubbornly hold on to our mistakes rather than seek forgiveness and change. This is another way that pride leads to destruction. Just as a mule's refusal to move can keep it from finding safety or help, pride's refusal to repent keeps us from experiencing God's mercy and grace. It keeps us stuck in our sin, unable to move forward in our relationship with God because we are too proud to admit that we need His forgiveness.

Pride also makes us stubborn in our relationships with others. Just as a mule refuses to budge, pride makes us unwilling to apologize or admit when we are wrong. This kind of stubbornness can cause rifts and divisions in our relationships, because it prevents reconciliation and healing. When we are too proud to say we're sorry, we allow pride to build walls between us and others. Instead of seeking to understand or repair the damage, pride makes us dig in our heels and insist that we were right, even if it means losing a friendship or damaging a relationship. This kind of stubbornness doesn't lead to peace or resolution; it leads to bitterness and division. Just as a mule's refusal to move can cause it to miss out on what it needs, pride's refusal to apologize or seek reconciliation causes us to miss out on the blessings of healthy relationships. It keeps us isolated, stuck in our own pride, unable to experience the joy and peace that comes from forgiveness and reconciliation.

Pride's stubbornness also makes it difficult for us to grow and learn. Just as a mule that refuses to move will never reach its destination, pride keeps us from growing spiritually, emotionally, and intellectually. When we are too proud to admit that we don't know everything or that we need help, we stop learning and growing. Pride tells us that asking for help is a sign of weakness, but the Bible teaches that humility is the path to wisdom. Proverbs 11:2 says, "When pride cometh, then cometh shame: but with the lowly is wisdom." True wisdom comes from being willing to admit that we don't have all the answers and that we need God's guidance and the support of others. But pride makes us stubbornly cling to our own understanding, even when it's clear that we need help. It makes us think that we can figure everything out on our own, but this kind of stubbornness only leads to frustration and failure. Just as a mule that refuses to move will never reach its destination, a person who is too proud to seek help or admit their limitations will never reach their full potential.

The Bible is full of warnings about the dangers of pride and stubbornness. Over and over again, we are reminded that pride leads to destruction, while humility leads to life. James 4:6 tells us, "But he giveth more grace. Wherefore he saith, God resisteth the proud, but giveth grace unto the humble." When we are filled with pride and stubbornly refuse to listen to correction, we are setting ourselves against God. We are resisting His guidance and His will for our lives. But when we humble ourselves and are willing to admit our faults, God gives us the grace we need to grow and change. He leads us on the right path and helps us overcome our weaknesses. Just as a mule needs its master to guide it, we need God to lead us. But pride makes us resist His leading. It makes us want to go our own way, even when that way leads to destruction.

In the end, pride's stubbornness is self-destructive. Just as a mule that refuses to move may miss out on food, water, or safety, a person who is filled with pride will miss out on the blessings that come from humility, repentance, and growth. Pride keeps us stuck in our ways, unable to move forward because we are too stubborn to admit that we need to change. It makes us blind to our own faults and resistant to the correction that could save us. But God, in His mercy, offers us a way out. He calls us to humble ourselves, to admit when we are wrong, and to seek His forgiveness and guidance. When we do this, we are no longer like the stubborn mule, refusing to move. Instead, we become like the humble servant, willing to be led by God and open to His correction. This is the path to true growth, wisdom, and life. Pride may be stubborn like a mule, but humility is the key to breaking free from that stubbornness and moving forward in our relationship with God and others. Just as a mule's stubbornness can be overcome with patience and guidance, our pride can be overcome when we humble ourselves before God and allow Him to lead us. Only then can we experience the fullness of life and the blessings that come from being teachable, repentant, and willing to grow.

Chapter 6 - Pride Hides Like A Serpent

Pride hides like a serpent, coiled up in the heart, waiting for the right moment to strike, just as a snake lies quietly in the grass, unnoticed, until it's ready to attack. Pride can slither into our lives without us realizing it, sneaking into our thoughts and attitudes, and before we know it, it has taken root deep within us. It doesn't always announce itself loudly or boldly; sometimes it remains hidden, quietly growing, waiting for the perfect opportunity to reveal itself in our actions and decisions. The Bible warns us about the danger of hidden pride, and Psalm 10:4 explains, "The wicked, through the pride of his countenance, will not seek after God: God is not in all his thoughts." This verse points to one of the most dangerous effects of pride—it causes us to turn away from God, to forget Him in our thoughts, and to rely on ourselves instead of seeking His guidance and help. Just like a serpent, pride hides in the heart, often unnoticed, until it begins to control our actions and pull us away from God.

The danger of pride is that it is so subtle. It can remain hidden for a long time, quietly influencing our choices and shaping our character, without us even realizing it. Like a serpent that stays still and quiet, blending into its surroundings, pride can blend into our daily lives, disguising itself as confidence, self-assurance, or independence. We may not see it at first, but pride begins to change the way we think and act. It makes us focus more on ourselves, on what we can accomplish, and on how others see us, rather than focusing on God and what He wants for our lives. Pride makes us self-centered, and the more we focus on ourselves, the more we push God out of our hearts and minds. When pride hides in our hearts, it slowly takes over, until God is no longer in our thoughts, and we begin to believe that we don't need Him. This is exactly what Psalm 10:4 warns about. Pride, like a serpent, coils itself around our thoughts, squeezing out our reliance on God, and filling us with a sense of self-sufficiency that leads us away from the Lord.

Pride often hides under the surface, disguised as something harmless, just as a serpent might appear to be a harmless creature until it strikes. It may start as a simple desire to do well, to succeed, or to be recognized for our efforts, but over time, these seemingly innocent desires can turn into something more dangerous. We begin to take too much pride in our achievements, our talents, or our knowledge. We start to think that we've earned everything we have on our own, without God's help. This is when pride starts to strike, just like a serpent that waits for the perfect moment to attack. It hides in our thoughts, convincing us that we are more important than we really are, that we don't need to rely on God as much as we used to, and that we can handle things on our own. The problem with pride is that it blinds us to the truth. Just like a snake can strike suddenly and unexpectedly, pride can suddenly reveal itself in our actions and attitudes, making us behave in ways that push us away from God and hurt our relationships with others.

Pride, when hidden like a serpent, doesn't always show itself right away. It lies quietly, waiting for the right moment to show its true nature. We might go through life thinking that everything is fine, not realizing that pride is lurking in our hearts, waiting for the chance to strike. Pride can hide behind good intentions, behind hard work, or even behind the desire to do what's right. But as it hides, it grows stronger, and eventually, it reveals itself in ways that are harmful to our spiritual lives. We stop seeking God as much as we used to. We stop praying as often, thinking that we've got everything under control. We stop reading His Word, thinking that we already know enough. And before we know it, pride has coiled itself around our hearts, and we no longer feel the need to rely on God. This is the hidden danger of pride. It creeps in slowly, without us even noticing, and then one day, we realize that we have drifted far from God because we allowed pride to take His place in our hearts.

Pride also hides by making us think that we are always right. Just as a serpent hides in the grass, pride hides in our opinions and beliefs, convincing us that our way of thinking is superior to others. It makes us stubborn, unwilling to listen to advice or correction, because we believe that we already have all the answers. This kind of pride is particularly dangerous because it isolates us from others and from God. We become so focused on proving that we are right, that we stop seeking God's guidance and stop being open to His correction. Proverbs 16:18 warns us that "Pride goeth before destruction, and an haughty spirit before a fall." When pride hides in our hearts, it sets us up for a fall, because it blinds us to the truth and makes us think that we don't need God's help or the help of others. Like a serpent that strikes suddenly, pride can lead to destruction in our lives, often when we least expect it.

Another way pride hides like a serpent is by convincing us that we are doing everything for the right reasons, even when our motives are actually selfish. Pride can disguise itself as ambition, as the desire to do well, or as the pursuit of excellence. But underneath these good intentions, pride is often lurking, waiting for the moment when we start to believe that our success is all because of our own efforts. When pride hides in this way, it makes us think that we deserve the credit for our achievements, rather than giving glory to God. This is dangerous because it shifts our focus away from God and onto ourselves. We start to think that we are the ones in control, that we are the ones making things happen, and that we don't need God as much as we thought. But the Bible reminds us that everything we have comes from God, and that without Him, we can do nothing (John 15:5). When pride hides in our hearts, it causes us to forget this truth, and we begin to take credit for things that are really the result of God's blessings and grace.

Pride also hides in the way we compare ourselves to others. Just like a serpent that hides in the shadows, pride hides in our thoughts when we start to look at others and think that we are better than they are. It convinces us that we are more talented, more successful, or more righteous than those around us, and it makes us feel superior. This kind of pride is especially harmful because it destroys relationships and creates division. It makes us look down on others, rather than seeing them as equals, loved by God. When pride hides in our hearts in this way, it prevents us from loving others the way God calls us to. It makes us selfish, focused on proving our own worth, rather than lifting others up and serving them with humility. Pride hides behind our comparisons, making us feel good about ourselves at the expense of others, but in doing so, it distances us from the love and grace of God.

The Bible is clear that pride is one of the most dangerous sins because it leads us away from God. When pride hides in our hearts, it keeps us from seeking God's guidance, from relying on His strength, and from acknowledging our need for Him. Psalm 10:4 reminds us that "The wicked, through the pride of his countenance, will not seek after God: God is not in all his thoughts." When pride takes over, it pushes God out of our minds and replaces Him with thoughts of our own greatness. We stop seeking Him because we think we don't need Him anymore. But the truth is, we need God every moment of every day. Without Him, we are lost, like sheep without a shepherd. Pride hides this truth from us, making us believe that we can handle life on our own, but this is a lie. We are completely dependent on God for everything, and when we allow pride to hide in our hearts, we are cutting ourselves off from the source of life and strength.

Pride, like a serpent, also hides in the small, everyday decisions we make. It can creep into our attitudes at work, at school, in our friendships, and even in our ministries. We may not notice it at first, but pride slowly starts to influence the way we think and act. We become more concerned with how others see us than with how God sees us. We start to seek approval from people rather than seeking approval from God. Pride makes us focus on our own image, on our reputation, and on our achievements, rather than focusing on serving God with humility. This hidden pride can lead us to make choices that are not in line with God's will, because we are more concerned with advancing our own plans than with following God's plan for our lives. Like a serpent that strikes unexpectedly, pride can lead us down a path of selfishness and sin, even when we don't realize it.

The only way to guard against the hidden danger of pride is through humility. Just as we would be cautious of a serpent hiding in the grass, we must be vigilant in guarding our hearts against pride. We must regularly examine our thoughts and attitudes, asking God to reveal any hidden pride and to help us root it out. The Bible tells us in James 4:6, "But he giveth more grace. Wherefore he saith, God resisteth the proud, but giveth grace unto the humble." When we humble ourselves before God, acknowledging our dependence on Him and our need for His guidance, He gives us the grace we need to overcome pride. Humility is the antidote to pride because it keeps us focused on God and reminds us that everything we have and everything we are comes from Him. When we walk in humility, pride

has no place to hide in our hearts, and we can live in the freedom of knowing that we are fully reliant on God's love and grace.

In conclusion, pride hides like a serpent, quietly coiling itself around our hearts and waiting for the moment to strike. It disguises itself as confidence, ambition, or self-sufficiency, but in reality, it is a dangerous sin that leads us away from God. When pride hides in our hearts, it blinds us to the truth, makes us rely on ourselves instead of on God, and damages our relationships with others. But when we humble ourselves and seek God's guidance, we can overcome the hidden danger of pride and live in the fullness of His grace and love.

Chapter 7 - Pride Claws Like A Bear

Pride claws like a bear, ready to lash out with fierce anger when it feels threatened or challenged. Just as a bear fiercely defends itself, especially when it believes its young are in danger, pride reacts aggressively when it is questioned or attacked. The Bible warns us about the destructive nature of pride, comparing it to a fool acting in folly, and in Proverbs 17:12, it says, "Let a bear robbed of her whelps meet a man, rather than a fool in his folly." This verse gives a vivid image of just how dangerous pride can be, because when a person is full of pride, their reactions are irrational and harmful, like a bear that is robbed of her cubs. Pride, like that enraged bear, does not think calmly or wisely. It does not seek peace or understanding. Instead, it seeks to defend itself at all costs, even if that means hurting others or causing destruction. When pride is threatened, it lashes out with claws of anger, sharp words, and stubborn resistance. It refuses to back down, to apologize, or to admit wrong, because to do so would be to admit vulnerability, and pride cannot stand the thought of being vulnerable.

When pride claws like a bear, it attacks in self-defense, often out of fear of losing control or power. Just as a bear claws to protect itself from perceived danger, pride claws to protect its image. When someone points out a fault, gives criticism, or challenges our opinions, pride feels attacked. It doesn't want to hear that we might be wrong, that we might need to change, or that we are not perfect. So instead of humbly accepting the correction, pride lashes out. It fights back with excuses, blame-shifting, or anger, trying to deflect the truth and maintain a sense of superiority. This defensive reaction is like a bear swiping its claws at anything that comes too close, even if that thing poses no real threat. Pride views any challenge to its image as an attack, and it responds with aggression, unwilling to show weakness or admit fault.

The problem with pride is that it blinds us to our own faults, making it difficult to accept correction. Just as a bear, in its rage, cannot see clearly or think rationally, pride clouds our judgment. It makes us defensive, quick to justify our actions, and slow to listen. Pride tells us that we are always right, that we don't need anyone else's advice or guidance, and that admitting wrong would make us look weak. But in reality, this defensive pride only makes us more foolish, as Proverbs 17:12 warns. It is better to face the danger of a bear than to deal with the stubbornness of a fool consumed by pride. A bear's attack might be deadly, but the damage caused by a prideful heart can be just as destructive, if not more so. Pride claws at relationships, tearing them apart with anger, hurtful words, and refusal to compromise or apologize. It claws at our spiritual growth, keeping us stuck in the same patterns of sin and stubbornness because we refuse to admit that we need to change.

Pride, like a bear with sharp claws, doesn't just lash out at others—it also causes harm to the person holding onto it. When pride claws defensively, it not only damages relationships with others, but it also harms our relationship with God. Pride makes us resistant to God's guidance and correction. Instead of humbly submitting to His will, pride causes us to dig in our heels and insist on our own way. This stubbornness is dangerous because it leads us further away from God and His plan for our lives. Just as a bear's claws can cause deep wounds, pride's defensiveness leaves scars on our hearts, keeping us from experiencing the healing and grace that God offers. Pride tells us that we don't need God's help, that we can handle things on our own, but this is a lie. In reality, pride's claws keep us from receiving the help and guidance we desperately need.

When pride is challenged, it reacts quickly, without thinking of the consequences. Like a bear that strikes out in a blind rage, pride lashes out impulsively, often hurting the people around us. It can cause us to say things we don't mean, to act out of anger or frustration, and to make decisions that we later regret. But pride doesn't care about the damage it causes in the moment. Its main concern is protecting itself, maintaining control, and defending its territory. It doesn't stop to consider the long-term effects of its actions. This is why pride is so dangerous. It leads to destructive behaviors, broken relationships, and a hardened heart. The Bible warns us in Proverbs 16:18, "Pride goeth before destruction, and an haughty spirit before a fall." When we allow pride to claw at our hearts, we are setting ourselves up for a fall. Just as a bear that attacks recklessly might end up getting hurt in the process, pride's defensive lashing out often backfires, causing more harm than good.

One of the most dangerous aspects of pride is that it makes us unwilling to admit when we are wrong. Just as a bear stubbornly fights to protect itself, pride refuses to back down or acknowledge fault. When we are full of pride, we resist apologizing, even when we know we've hurt someone. We justify our actions, make excuses, or blame others, all in an effort to avoid admitting that we were wrong. But this kind of stubborn pride only leads to more conflict and division. Instead of bringing healing, pride's claws dig deeper into the wound, making it harder to repair the damage. The longer we hold onto pride, the more it grows, and the harder it becomes to let go. Just like a bear that becomes more aggressive when threatened, pride becomes more entrenched the more it is challenged. It makes us defensive, argumentative, and unwilling to listen to others, which only drives people further away.

Pride also claws at our ability to grow and learn. Just as a bear's defensive instincts prevent it from seeing clearly or thinking rationally, pride prevents us from learning from our mistakes. When pride is in control, we are more focused on protecting our image than on growing as individuals. We don't want to admit that we have room for improvement, because that would mean acknowledging our imperfections. But growth requires humility. It requires the willingness to admit that we don't have all the answers, that we make mistakes, and that we need to change. Pride, on the other hand, keeps us stuck in a cycle of defensiveness and denial. It claws at our potential, holding us back from becoming the people God created us to be. Just as a bear's claws can tear through flesh, pride tears through our opportunities for growth and transformation, leaving us stagnant and resistant to change.

Pride's defensiveness also makes it difficult for us to accept help from others. Just as a bear might refuse to let anyone come close out of fear of being harmed, pride causes us to push people away when they try to offer help or guidance. We don't want to appear weak or dependent on others, so we reject their advice or assistance. But this kind of pride is foolish, because none of us can go through life alone. We all need support, encouragement, and wisdom from others, and most importantly, we need God's help. But when pride claws at our hearts, we close ourselves off from the people who could help us and from the God who wants to guide us. Instead of reaching out for help, we stubbornly try to handle everything on our own, even when we are struggling. This kind of pride is not strength; it is weakness disguised as strength. It is the bear that refuses to let anyone near, even when it is wounded and in need of help.

The Bible teaches that humility, not pride, is the path to wisdom and peace. James 4:6 reminds us, "But he giveth more grace. Wherefore he saith, God resisteth the proud, but giveth grace unto the humble." When we humble ourselves before God and before others, we open ourselves up to the grace and guidance that can transform our lives. But pride's claws keep us from receiving that grace. They make us believe that we don't need it, that we are fine on our own, and that admitting weakness would make us less valuable. But the truth is, humility is the key to true strength and wisdom. When we let go of pride and admit our need for God's help, we experience His grace in ways we never could when we were holding onto pride. Just as a bear that stops fighting and trusts its master is better off than one that continues to struggle, we are better off when we let go of our pride and trust God to lead us.

In relationships, pride's claws can cause deep wounds, but humility has the power to heal. When pride is challenged, it lashes out defensively, but humility responds with grace and understanding. When someone criticizes us or points out a fault, pride reacts with anger or denial, but humility listens, reflects, and seeks to grow. This is why humility is so important in maintaining healthy relationships. It allows us to admit when we are wrong, to apologize sincerely, and to seek reconciliation. Pride, on the other hand, keeps us stuck in conflict, refusing to back down or admit fault. Just as a bear's claws can cause serious injury, pride can cause serious damage to our relationships. But when we choose humility over pride, we create space for healing, growth, and deeper connection with others.

Ultimately, pride's defensive nature is a sign of insecurity. Just as a bear claws to protect itself when it feels threatened, pride lashes out because it is afraid of being exposed. Pride doesn't want to show weakness or vulnerability, so it fights back with anger, denial, and stubbornness. But true strength comes from humility, from being willing to admit our imperfections and seek help when we need it. When we let go of pride's claws and embrace humility, we find peace, wisdom, and the grace of God. We no longer feel the need to defend ourselves at all costs, because we trust that God is in control and that His grace is sufficient for us.

In conclusion, pride claws like a bear, lashing out defensively when it feels threatened or challenged. It reacts with anger, stubbornness, and denial, causing harm to our relationships, our spiritual growth, and our relationship with God. Just as a bear's claws can cause deep wounds, pride's defensive nature can leave lasting scars. But the Bible teaches that humility is the path to peace and wisdom. When we humble ourselves before God and others, we let go of pride's claws and open ourselves to the grace, healing, and guidance that can transform our lives. Pride may claw fiercely, but humility brings the peace and strength that pride can never offer.

Chapter 8 -Pride Slithers Like A Snake

Pride slithers like a snake, moving subtly through our hearts and minds, often deceiving us with its presence and intentions. Just as a snake slithers quietly through the grass, almost invisible, pride sneaks into our lives without us even realizing it. It doesn't announce itself loudly or boldly, but rather, it creeps in, slowly wrapping itself around our thoughts and actions. Pride, like a serpent, is crafty and deceitful. It can make us believe that we are simply confident, self-assured, or standing up for what we deserve, when in reality, it is leading us down a dangerous path. In Genesis 3:1, we see the subtlety of the serpent in the Garden of Eden, where it deceived Eve with half-truths and lies. "Now the serpent was more subtil than any beast of the field which the Lord God had made. And he said unto the woman, Yea, hath God said, Ye shall not eat of every tree of the garden?" the Bible says. This subtle, cunning nature of the serpent is much like the nature of pride. Pride often disguises itself as something good, making us believe that it is harmless, but it is a trap that leads us away from God and into sin.

The danger of pride is that it often goes unnoticed at first. It doesn't strike suddenly or violently like other sins might; instead, it slithers in slowly, blending in with our thoughts and desires. It begins with a small feeling of superiority, a subtle thought that we are better than others in some way. Maybe it's in our abilities, our intelligence, our looks, or our status. We might not even recognize it as pride at first, because it feels like confidence or self-assurance. But as it slithers deeper into our hearts, pride starts to take over, and before we know it, it has coiled itself around us, tightening its grip. Just as a snake hides in the grass, waiting for the right moment to strike, pride hides in the corners of our hearts, waiting for the moment when we are most vulnerable. It waits until we are comfortable, until we feel secure in ourselves, and then it strikes, making us believe that we don't need God as much as we thought we did.

One of the most dangerous aspects of pride is its ability to deceive. Like a snake that strikes without warning, pride deceives us into thinking that we are more important or more capable than we really are. It makes us believe that we have everything under control, that we don't need help from others, and that we don't need to rely on God. Pride tells us that we can handle life on our own, that we deserve praise and recognition for our accomplishments, and that we are the ones who make things happen. But this is a lie. The Bible teaches us that everything we have comes from God, and without Him, we can do nothing (John 15:5). Pride, however, slithers into our minds and convinces us that we are self-sufficient, that we can take credit for our successes, and that we don't need to acknowledge God's role in our lives. This deception is dangerous because it pulls us away from God and leads us into a false sense of security, where we believe that we are in control when, in reality, we are not.

Pride also slithers into our relationships with others, deceiving us into thinking that we are better than those around us. It makes us compare ourselves to others, and instead of seeing them as equals, we start to see them as competitors. Pride whispers in our ear, telling us that we are smarter, more talented, or more deserving than the people around us. It makes us feel superior, and this superiority leads to division and conflict. We stop listening to others, we stop valuing their opinions, and we start to believe that our way is the only right way. Pride deceives us into thinking that we don't need to consider others' feelings or perspectives because we are always right. This kind of pride destroys relationships, because it creates a barrier between us and others. Just as a snake slithers between rocks and crevices, separating itself from its surroundings, pride separates us from the people we care about, making it difficult to connect with them on a deeper level.

Pride not only affects our relationships with others, but it also affects our relationship with God. Like the serpent in the Garden of Eden, pride slithers into our hearts, tempting us to disobey God and follow our own desires. In Genesis 3:1, the serpent deceived Eve by making her question God's command, saying, "Now the serpent was more subtil than any beast of the field which the Lord God had made. And he said unto the woman, Yea, hath God said, Ye shall not eat of every tree of the garden?" Pride does the same thing to us. It makes us question God's authority and His commands. It tells us that we know better than God, that we can make our own decisions without His guidance, and that we don't need to follow His rules because we are capable of figuring things out on our own. This kind of thinking is dangerous because it leads us away from God's will for our lives. When pride slithers in, we stop seeking God's wisdom and start relying on our own understanding, which ultimately leads to destruction.

The Bible warns us repeatedly about the dangers of pride and the need for humility. Proverbs 16:18 says, "Pride goeth before destruction, and an haughty spirit before a fall." Just as a snake's bite can be deadly, pride's deception can lead to our downfall if we are not careful. Pride makes us believe that we are invincible, that we can handle anything that comes our way, but this is a dangerous illusion. When we rely on our own strength and refuse to humble ourselves before God, we are setting ourselves up for failure. Pride blinds us to our own weaknesses and faults, making it difficult for us to see where we need to grow and change. Just as a snake hides in the shadows, pride hides our flaws from us, keeping us from acknowledging them and seeking God's help to overcome them.

Pride also slithers into our spiritual lives, deceiving us into thinking that we are more righteous or holier than others. It makes us believe that because we go to church, read the Bible, or do good deeds, we are somehow better than those who don't. But this kind of spiritual pride is just as dangerous as any other form of pride. It blinds us to the truth that we are all sinners in need of God's grace. Romans 3:23 reminds us, "For all have sinned, and come short of the glory of God." Pride makes us forget this truth and leads us to judge others harshly, thinking that we are more deserving of God's love and favor. But the Bible teaches us that God resists the proud and gives grace to the humble (James 4:6). When we allow pride to slither into our spiritual lives, we are cutting ourselves off from the grace and mercy that God offers to those who humble themselves before Him.

The subtlety of pride makes it one of the most difficult sins to recognize and overcome. Just as a snake moves quietly and carefully, pride often goes unnoticed until it has already done its damage. We may not realize that pride has taken root in our hearts until we find ourselves acting out of arrogance, selfishness, or a desire for control. Pride can manifest in many different ways—through our words, our actions, and even our thoughts. It can show up in the way we treat others, the way we respond to criticism, and the way we handle success. But no matter how pride reveals itself, it always leads us away from God and into sin. This is why it is so important to be vigilant in guarding our hearts against pride. We must regularly examine ourselves, asking God to reveal any hidden pride and help us to root it out before it takes control.

The only way to overcome pride is through humility. Just as a snake is powerless when it is exposed to the light, pride loses its power when we humble ourselves before God. Humility is the antidote to pride because it keeps us focused on God's greatness rather than our own. When we humble ourselves, we acknowledge that we are nothing without God, that we need His guidance and strength in every aspect of our lives. Philippians 2:3-4 says, "Let nothing be done through strife or vainglory; but in lowliness of mind let each esteem other better than themselves. Look not every man on his own things, but every man also on the things of others." Humility helps us to put others before ourselves, to serve rather than to be served, and to seek God's will above our own. When we walk in humility, pride has no place to slither in and take hold of our hearts.

In conclusion, pride slithers like a snake, moving subtly and deceptively through our hearts and minds. It disguises itself as confidence, self-assurance, or independence, but in reality, it is a dangerous sin that leads us away from God and into destruction. Just as the serpent deceived Eve in the Garden of Eden, pride deceives us into thinking that we don't need God, that we can handle life on our own, and that we are better than those around us. But the Bible warns us that pride leads to destruction and that God resists the proud but gives grace to the humble. The only way to overcome the slithering nature of pride is through humility, by acknowledging our need for God and putting others before ourselves. Just as light exposes a snake and renders it powerless, humility exposes pride and takes away its control over our lives. When we humble ourselves before God, we open our hearts to His grace, wisdom, and guidance, and we protect ourselves from the subtle, deceptive grip of pride.

Chapter 9 - Pride Digs Like A Mole

Pride digs like a mole, burrowing deep within our hearts and minds, often hard to detect, hiding beneath the surface until it suddenly emerges in our behaviors and attitudes. Just as a mole tunnels quietly underground, making its way through the soil without anyone noticing, pride works its way into our lives in ways that are not always obvious at first. It settles into the deepest parts of who we are, quietly shaping our thoughts, feelings, and actions until it finally reveals itself in the way we treat others, in the way we see ourselves, and in the way we approach God. The Bible warns us about the dangers of pride, particularly in the book of Obadiah, where we read in Obadiah 1:3, "The pride of thine heart hath deceived thee, thou that dwellest in the clefts of the rock, whose habitation is high; that saith in his heart, Who shall bring me down to the ground?" This verse highlights how pride can deceive us, making us feel secure, powerful, and untouchable, much like someone living high up in the clefts of a rock. Pride digs deep, convincing us that we are safe in our own strength, in our own accomplishments, and in our own wisdom. But this sense of security is a lie. Just like a mole that burrows underground, pride stays hidden for a while, but eventually, it will surface, and when it does, it brings destruction with it.

The subtlety of pride is what makes it so dangerous. It doesn't come crashing into our lives with loud and obvious signs. Instead, it sneaks in, much like a mole burrows silently beneath the ground. At first, we might not even realize that pride has taken root in our hearts. It starts small, with a thought here or an attitude there—maybe we begin to feel a little more important than others because of something we've accomplished, or maybe we start to think we're more righteous because of the good things we've done. These thoughts seem harmless at first, but over time, pride digs deeper. It burrows into our thoughts, shaping the way we see ourselves and the world around us. Slowly, pride convinces us that we are better than others, that we deserve more recognition, or that we have achieved everything on our own. Like a mole that digs deep tunnels underground, pride creates pathways in our hearts that are hard to detect, but these pathways lead to a false sense of security and self-reliance that ultimately separates us from God.

One of the most deceptive aspects of pride is how it makes us feel invincible. Just as someone living in the clefts of a high rock might feel safe and untouchable, pride makes us feel like we are above the dangers that others face. It convinces us that we don't need to rely on God as much as others do, that we have everything under control, and that we can handle life on our own. Pride digs deep, creating a foundation of self-reliance and arrogance that makes us think we are untouchable. But the Bible tells us that this kind of pride is deceptive. In Obadiah 1:3, God speaks to the people who dwell in the high places, warning them that their pride has deceived them. They may feel secure, but their pride will be their downfall. Pride, like a mole digging deep underground, creates a false sense of safety. It burrows deep into our hearts, convincing us that we are secure in our own abilities, our own knowledge, or our own achievements. But just as a mole's tunnels can weaken the ground and cause it to collapse, pride weakens the foundation of our lives, and eventually, it will cause us to fall.

Pride doesn't just deceive us about our own strength and abilities—it also deceives us about our need for God. Just as a mole hides underground, pride hides the truth from us, making us believe that we don't need God's help or guidance as much as we actually do. It makes us think that we can figure things out on our own, that we can solve our own problems, and that we don't need to rely on God for every aspect of our lives. This kind of pride digs deep into our hearts, cutting us off from the very source of life and strength that we need. When pride burrows into our hearts, it creates a barrier between us and God. We stop seeking Him in prayer as often, we stop reading His Word with the same hunger for wisdom, and we stop relying on His guidance in our daily decisions. Instead, pride makes us turn inward, relying on our own understanding and our own strength. But the Bible warns us in Proverbs 3:5-6 to "Trust in the Lord with all thine heart; and lean not unto thine own understanding. In all thy ways acknowledge him, and he shall direct thy paths." Pride, however, digs deep within us and convinces us to do the opposite—to lean on our own understanding, to trust in ourselves, and to think that we don't need God as much as we once did.

Another way that pride digs deep like a mole is in how it affects our relationships with others. Just as a mole burrows beneath the surface, pride often hides beneath our outward actions and words, but it eventually surfaces in the way we treat those around us. Pride can make us impatient with others, especially when we feel that they are not as capable or as knowledgeable as we are. It can make us look down on people who struggle in areas where we succeed, and it can cause us to dismiss the opinions or ideas of others because we believe we know better. Pride digs into our hearts, creating attitudes of superiority and self-righteousness that damage our relationships. We may not realize it at first, but pride slowly erodes our ability to empathize with others, to listen to their concerns, and to value their perspectives. Instead, we become more focused on proving ourselves right, on getting our way, or on receiving recognition for our own achievements. This kind of pride destroys the humility and love that are essential for healthy relationships.

The Bible teaches us that humility, not pride, is the key to building strong, loving relationships. In Philippians 2:3, we are told, "Let nothing be done through strife or vainglory; but in lowliness of mind let each esteem other better than themselves." But when pride digs deep into our hearts, it makes this kind of humility difficult, if not impossible. Pride convinces us that we are better than others, that we deserve more recognition, and that we shouldn't have to lower ourselves to serve or listen to those around us. This attitude not only harms our relationships with others, but it also harms our relationship with God. Just as pride digs deep tunnels that separate us from others, it also digs deep tunnels that separate us from God. The more pride burrows into our hearts, the more distant we become from Him, because pride convinces us that we don't need Him as much as we once thought we did.

Pride also digs deep within us by making us blind to our own faults and weaknesses. Just as a mole burrows underground, out of sight, pride hides our flaws from us, making it difficult for us to see where we need to grow or change. It makes us focus on the faults of others instead, constantly pointing out where they are wrong or where they need to improve, while ignoring our own shortcomings. This kind of pride is dangerous because it keeps us from recognizing our need for repentance and transformation. The Bible tells us in James 4:6, "But he giveth more grace. Wherefore he saith, God resisteth the proud, but giveth grace unto the humble." When pride digs deep into our hearts, we resist the grace that God offers because we are unwilling to admit that we need it. We become so focused on defending our own righteousness that we miss the opportunity to receive God's forgiveness and healing. Just as a mole's tunnels can cause damage to the ground above, pride's deep roots cause damage to our spiritual lives, preventing us from experiencing the fullness of God's grace and mercy.

The only way to overcome the deep-rooted nature of pride is through humility. Just as a mole's tunnels need to be uncovered and filled in to prevent further damage, the pride that digs deep into our hearts needs to be exposed and rooted out. This begins with a willingness to admit that we are not as self-sufficient as we may think we are. It requires us to humble ourselves before God, acknowledging that we need His help in every area of our lives. In Micah 6:8, we are reminded of what God requires of us: "He hath shewed thee, O man, what is good; and what doth the Lord require of thee, but to do justly, and to love mercy, and to walk humbly with thy God?" Walking humbly with God means recognizing that we are dependent on Him for everything, that we are not above His correction, and that we need His grace every day.

Humility also requires us to be honest with ourselves about our own faults and weaknesses. Just as a mole's tunnels need to be exposed to the light in order to be dealt with, the pride that burrows into our hearts needs to be brought into the light of God's truth. This means being willing to admit when we are wrong, being open to correction from others, and being quick to repent when we fall short. It means letting go of the need to always be right, to always be in control, and to always receive recognition. Instead, humility calls us to serve others, to put their needs before our own, and to give glory to God for everything we have and everything we accomplish.

In conclusion, pride digs like a mole, burrowing deep within our hearts, often hard to detect, until it surfaces in our behaviors and attitudes. It deceives us into believing that we are self-sufficient, that we don't need God as much as we once thought, and that we are better than those around us. Pride creates a false sense of security, convincing us that we are untouchable, but in reality, it weakens the foundation of our lives and leads to destruction. The Bible warns us about the dangers of pride and calls us to walk in humility, recognizing our dependence on God and our need for His grace. Just as a mole's tunnels need to be uncovered and filled in to prevent further damage, the pride that digs deep into our hearts needs to be exposed and rooted out through humility, repentance, and a willingness to seek God's guidance in all things. When we humble ourselves before God, we allow Him to fill in the tunnels of pride with His grace, love, and truth, and we begin to walk in the freedom and peace that only comes from living a life fully surrendered to Him.

Chapter 10 - Pride Parades Like A Horse In Battle

Pride parades like a horse in battle, eager to charge forward, full of energy, strength, and determination, but often without consideration of the consequences. Like a warhorse ready to rush into the fight, pride drives us ahead with reckless abandon, making us think we are invincible, unstoppable, and in control of everything. The Bible tells us in Proverbs 21:31, "The horse is prepared against the day of battle: but safety is of the Lord." This verse reminds us that no matter how strong or prepared we may feel, true safety and victory come only from the Lord, not from our own strength or efforts. Yet pride makes us forget this truth. It pushes us forward, much like a horse that charges into battle without thinking of what lies ahead—danger, obstacles, or even defeat. Pride makes us overconfident, causing us to trust in our own abilities, our own plans, and our own understanding, rather than seeking the guidance and protection of God. Just as a horse in battle can be blinded by the adrenaline and excitement of the fight, pride blinds us to the dangers ahead, making us unaware of the potential consequences of our actions.

When pride parades like a horse in battle, it fills us with a sense of invincibility. We feel as though we can take on anything, overcome any challenge, and achieve anything we set our minds to. While confidence in our abilities is important, pride takes this confidence too far, turning it into arrogance and self-reliance. Instead of trusting in God's strength, we start to trust in our own. Pride tells us that we don't need God's help, that we are strong enough to handle life's battles on our own. Like a horse charging into battle without a rider to guide it, we charge forward without seeking God's wisdom or direction. We believe that our plans are foolproof, that our goals are always right, and that nothing can stand in our way. But the Bible warns us that pride leads to destruction. Proverbs 16:18 tells us, "Pride goeth before destruction, and an haughty spirit before a fall." Just as a horse in battle may stumble and fall if it charges recklessly, we are at risk of falling when we let pride take control and refuse to seek God's guidance.

Pride not only makes us overconfident, but it also makes us impatient. Like a horse that is eager to charge into battle, pride pushes us to rush ahead without waiting for God's timing. We become so focused on achieving our goals or proving ourselves that we forget to pause and seek God's will for our lives. We want to move forward, to advance, to succeed, and we become frustrated when things don't happen as quickly as we would like. Pride tells us that we should be able to make things happen on our own, without waiting on God. It makes us believe that our timing is better than His, and that if we just push hard enough, we can force things to go our way. But the Bible teaches us that waiting on the Lord is essential for true success. Psalm 27:14 says, "Wait on the Lord: be of good courage, and he shall strengthen thine heart: wait, I say, on the Lord." Pride, however, makes it difficult for us to wait. It urges us to charge ahead like a horse in battle, driven by our own desires and plans, rather than trusting in God's perfect timing.

Another way that pride parades like a horse in battle is by making us focus on outward appearances and achievements. Just as a warhorse is often adorned with armor and decorations to display its strength and power, pride causes us to focus on how we appear to others. We want to be seen as strong, successful, and important. Pride makes us parade our accomplishments, seeking the approval and admiration of others. We become more concerned with how others perceive us than with what God thinks of us. Pride pushes us to show off our successes, to boast about our achievements, and to seek recognition for what we have done. But the Bible warns against this kind of prideful display. In Galatians 6:3, we are told, "For if a man think himself to be something, when he is nothing, he deceiveth himself." Pride deceives us into believing that our worth is tied to our accomplishments and the approval of others, but true worth comes from our relationship with God, not from how we are perceived by the world.

Pride also parades in the way it makes us want to take control of our own destiny. Like a horse that charges into battle, trusting in its own strength and speed, pride makes us believe that we are in control of our own future. It tells us that we can plan our own path, that we can achieve anything if we work hard enough, and that we don't need to rely on God's guidance. Pride makes us think that we are the masters of our own fate, but this is a dangerous lie. The Bible teaches us that while we may make plans, it is ultimately God who directs our steps. Proverbs 19:21 says, "There are many devices in a man's heart; nevertheless the counsel of the Lord, that shall stand." Pride, however, makes us believe that we are in control, that we don't need to submit our plans to God, and that we can achieve success on our own terms. But just as a horse in battle can be thrown off course by obstacles it didn't anticipate, we too can be thrown off course when we rely on our own strength and wisdom rather than trusting in God's plan for our lives.

Pride's desire to charge ahead without considering the consequences can also lead to conflict and division in our relationships. Like a horse in battle that charges forward without regard for what it might trample in its path, pride causes us to rush ahead in our interactions with others, often without thinking about how our words or actions might affect them. Pride makes us want to be right, to win arguments, and to prove our point, even if it means hurting those around us. It causes us to speak before we think, to act without considering the feelings of others, and to push our own agenda without listening to the perspectives of those around us. This kind of pride creates division, because it prioritizes our own desires and opinions over the needs and concerns of others. The Bible teaches us to pursue peace and unity in our relationships, not to charge ahead with prideful ambitions. In Romans 12:18, we are instructed, "If it be possible, as much as lieth in you, live peaceably with all men." But pride, like a horse in battle, often leads us to do the opposite, creating conflict and discord instead of peace.

Pride's eagerness to charge ahead without consideration of the consequences can also have a profound impact on our spiritual lives. Just as a horse in battle may be driven by adrenaline and excitement, pride can make us driven by our own desires and ambitions, causing us to lose sight of what is truly important—our relationship with God. When we allow pride to take the reins, we become more focused on achieving our own goals, on proving ourselves, and on being successful in the eyes of the world, rather than seeking to grow closer to God and follow His will for our lives. Pride makes us want to charge ahead in our own strength, rather than humbly submitting to God's guidance and trusting in His plan. This kind of pride leads to spiritual burnout, because we are constantly striving and pushing forward in our own strength, rather than resting in God's grace and relying on His power.

The Bible teaches us that humility, not pride, is the path to true success and peace. In James 4:10, we are told, "Humble yourselves in the sight of the Lord, and he shall lift you up." When we humble ourselves before God, we acknowledge that we are not in control, that we cannot achieve success on our own, and that we need His guidance and strength in every aspect of our lives. Humility allows us to step back and let God take the lead, rather than charging ahead like a horse in battle, driven by pride. It reminds us that true success is not measured by our achievements or by how others perceive us, but by our faithfulness to God and our willingness to submit to His will.

Humility also helps us to maintain healthy relationships with others, because it allows us to listen, to consider the feelings and perspectives of those around us, and to seek peace rather than conflict. When we are humble, we are more willing to admit when we are wrong, to apologize when we have hurt someone, and to prioritize the needs of others over our own prideful desires. This kind of humility fosters unity and love, rather than the division and conflict that pride often creates.

In conclusion, pride parades like a horse in battle, charging ahead with reckless abandon, eager to prove itself, but often without consideration of the consequences. It makes us overconfident, impatient, and focused on outward appearances and achievements, rather than on our relationship with God and the well-being of those around us. Pride deceives us into thinking that we are in control, that we can achieve success on our own, and that we don't need to rely on God's guidance or submit to His will. But the Bible teaches us that true safety and success come not from our own strength, but from the Lord. When we humble ourselves before God, we allow Him to take the lead, trusting in His plan and His timing, rather than charging ahead in our own prideful ambitions. Just as a horse in battle needs a rider to guide it, we need God to guide us, to protect us, and to lead us to victory—not in our own strength, but in His. Pride may parade boldly, but humility walks wisely, and it is through humility that we find true peace, success, and fulfillment in the Lord.

Chapter 11 - Pride Multiplies Like A Pack Of Wolves

Pride multiplies like a pack of wolves, spreading quickly and aggressively, bringing with it a host of other sinful attitudes that only grow stronger and more destructive over time. Once pride takes root in our hearts, it doesn't stay confined to just one area of our lives. Like wolves hunting in packs, pride moves through every part of us, multiplying its influence and feeding on other weaknesses, turning them into a greater danger. Isaiah 56:11 states "Yea, they are greedy dogs which can never have enough, and they are shepherds that cannot understand: they all look to their own way, every one for his gain, from his quarter." The Bible paints a picture of greed and selfishness, comparing them to greedy dogs who "can never have enough" and to shepherds who have lost their way, looking only for their own gain. This description captures the essence of what pride does once it takes hold. Pride, like those greedy dogs, is never satisfied. It always wants more—more praise, more recognition, more power, more control. And as it spreads, pride brings with it a pack of other sinful attitudes: greed, envy, anger, selfishness, and arrogance, all working together to lead us further from God and deeper into sin.

At first, pride may seem small, like a single wolf, something we can control or ignore. We might think that a little pride is harmless, that it's just confidence or ambition. But pride is deceptive. It quickly grows, gathering more and more sinful thoughts and behaviors into its pack, until it overwhelms us. Like a pack of wolves hunting together, pride and the sins it attracts begin to work together to destroy the good in us. What started as a small sense of pride in our accomplishments can soon lead to selfishness, where we begin to think only of ourselves and our own desires. Then, as selfishness takes hold, it breeds greed, the desire to have more than we need or deserve, and soon we find ourselves consumed by envy, wishing we had what others possess. Pride feeds these attitudes, making them stronger and more powerful, just as a pack of wolves grows bolder and more dangerous when they hunt together.

Pride, once it multiplies, becomes harder to recognize and even harder to control. Like wolves that multiply in the wild, pride spreads quickly, and before we know it, it has invaded every part of our lives. It can affect the way we think about ourselves, convincing us that we are more important than others or that we deserve more recognition for our achievements. It can affect the way we treat others, making us harsh, critical, and unkind as we begin to see people as obstacles to our own success. Pride can even affect our relationship with God, as it grows into a sense of self-reliance, convincing us that we don't need God's guidance or grace because we can handle things on our own. This is why pride is so dangerous. Like a pack of wolves that surrounds its prey, pride surrounds us, attacking from every angle, using our own weaknesses against us. The more pride grows, the more isolated we become from God and from the people around us.

When pride multiplies like a pack of wolves, it also brings with it a hunger for more—more power, more control, more success. Isaiah 56:11 describes people who are greedy, never satisfied, always wanting more for themselves, and this is exactly what pride does to us. Pride makes us feel like we are never good enough unless we have more—more recognition, more possessions, more achievements. It pushes us to constantly compare ourselves to others, always measuring our worth by how much better we are than those around us. But this kind of pride only leads to more dissatisfaction. No matter how much we achieve or how much we gain, it is never enough. Pride, like a pack of wolves that can never be satisfied, keeps pushing us to want more, to take more, to demand more, without ever stopping to appreciate what we already have. It creates a vicious cycle where we are always striving, always hungry for more, but never truly fulfilled.

The greed that pride brings is particularly dangerous because it leads to other sins like envy and dishonesty. When pride makes us crave more for ourselves, we begin to look at what others have and feel jealous. We want what they have, and pride tells us that we deserve it more than they do. This envy can lead us to make bad decisions, to lie or cheat in order to get ahead, or to harm others in our pursuit of success. Just as a pack of wolves will attack and overpower anything that stands in its way, pride drives us to push aside anything—or anyone—that gets between us and what we want. This selfishness destroys relationships, ruins our integrity, and leaves us spiritually bankrupt, because we are no longer living according to God's will but according to our own selfish desires.

Pride also multiplies in our hearts by making us blind to our own faults. Just as a pack of wolves moves stealthily through the night, pride works quietly within us, making it difficult to see the damage it is causing. It deceives us into thinking that we are always right, that our way is the best way, and that we don't need to listen to the advice or correction of others. Isaiah 56:11 speaks of shepherds who cannot understand, and this can happen to us when pride takes over. We lose the ability to understand or see clearly because pride clouds our judgment. We become so focused on our own needs and desires that we can no longer see the truth about ourselves. We stop examining our own hearts, and instead, we point out the flaws in others. We become critical, judgmental, and self-righteous, believing that we are superior to those around us. But in reality, pride is leading us down a dangerous path, one where we are cut off from the wisdom and guidance that God offers.

Pride's multiplication doesn't just affect us individually—it can spread to those around us, influencing our families, our communities, and even our churches. Just as wolves travel and hunt in packs, pride can spread from one person to another, creating an atmosphere of selfishness, competition, and division. When pride takes hold in a group of people, it creates conflict, because everyone is focused on their own interests rather than working together for the good of others. In a family, pride can cause arguments, bitterness, and resentment as each person tries to prove that they are right or that they deserve more respect. In a community, pride can lead to division, as people become more concerned with their own success or status than with supporting and helping one another. And in a church, pride can destroy unity, as people begin to compete for recognition or power, rather than serving God and each other with humility. This is why pride is so destructive—it multiplies, infecting not just one person but entire groups, tearing apart the bonds of love and unity that God calls us to build.

The Bible teaches us that humility, not pride, is the key to overcoming the destructive power of sin. In Philippians 2:3, we are told, "Let nothing be done through strife or vainglory; but in lowliness of mind let each esteem other better than themselves." Humility is the opposite of pride. While pride multiplies selfishness, greed, and arrogance, humility multiplies love, kindness, and service. Humility allows us to see ourselves and others as God sees us—not as competitors, but as beloved children of God, each valuable and worthy of respect. When we choose humility, we break the power of pride and stop it from multiplying in our hearts. Instead of seeking our own gain, we begin to seek the good of others. Instead of striving for more recognition or power, we begin to serve others with a heart of love and generosity.

Humility also opens the door for God's grace to work in our lives. James 4:6 tells us, "But he giveth more grace. Wherefore he saith, God resisteth the proud, but giveth grace unto the humble." When we humble ourselves before God, we acknowledge that we cannot do everything on our own, that we need His guidance, His wisdom, and His strength. Humility allows us to rely on God's power, rather than our own, and it gives us the grace to overcome the sins that pride brings into our lives. It is through humility that we find true peace, joy, and fulfillment, because we are no longer chasing after the empty promises of pride, but we are resting in the love and provision of God.

In conclusion, pride multiplies like a pack of wolves, spreading quickly and aggressively, bringing other sinful attitudes along with it. It starts small, but once it takes root, it grows and spreads, leading to greed, envy, selfishness, and arrogance. Pride makes us hungry for more—more power, more recognition, more control—just like a pack of wolves that can never be satisfied. It blinds us to our own faults, making us critical of others and unable to see the damage it is causing in our lives. But the Bible warns us that pride leads to destruction, and it calls us to embrace humility instead. When we humble ourselves before God, we stop pride from multiplying in our hearts, and we allow God's grace to fill us with love, kindness, and service. Humility breaks the power of pride, allowing us to live in peace and unity with others, and to experience the fullness of God's love and blessings. Just as a pack of wolves can be dangerous and destructive, so too is pride when it is left unchecked. But with humility, we can overcome pride and live lives that honor God and reflect His love to the world.

Chapter 12 - Pride Stings Like A Scorpion

Pride stings like a scorpion, its bite sharp and painful, leaving behind wounds that can harm not only oneself but also others. Just as a scorpion's sting injects venom into its victim, pride injects toxic attitudes and behaviors into our hearts and minds, affecting our relationships, our actions, and our spiritual well-being. The consequences of pride, like the sting of a scorpion, are often unexpected and severe. They hurt us deeply and can linger for a long time, causing damage that is difficult to heal. Revelation 9:10 paints a vivid picture of the harm that pride and other sins can cause, saying, "And they had tails like unto scorpions, and there were stings in their tails: and their power was to hurt men five months." The sting of a scorpion is not a brief or fleeting pain—it endures, and so does the pain caused by pride. Whether through broken relationships, damaged reputations, or spiritual downfall, the sting of pride leaves lasting effects that can take months, years, or even a lifetime to fully heal.

Pride's sting is sharp because it blinds us to the truth, making us believe that we are always right, that we are better than others, or that we are in control of our own destiny. This deception leads us into dangerous territory, where we make decisions based on arrogance and self-importance rather than humility and wisdom. Pride, like a scorpion ready to strike, waits for the moment when we are most vulnerable—when we are filled with confidence in ourselves, when we feel invincible or untouchable—and then it delivers its sting. The pain of pride often comes from the consequences of our own actions. When we act out of pride, we hurt others by being dismissive, arrogant, or unkind, and in doing so, we damage our relationships. Pride makes us say things we shouldn't say, act in ways that are selfish, and ignore the needs or feelings of those around us. The sting of pride is especially painful because it often leads to regret. Once the damage is done, we look back and realize how pride caused us to hurt others or to make choices that were not in line with God's will, and that realization stings deeply.

The sting of pride doesn't only hurt others; it also harms us. Just as a scorpion's venom can cause physical pain, pride's sting causes emotional and spiritual pain. When we allow pride to control our hearts, we separate ourselves from God's guidance and grace. We become more focused on our own desires, our own success, and our own image than on seeking God's will for our lives. This separation from God leads to emptiness, frustration, and a sense of dissatisfaction, because pride can never truly fulfill us. Pride tells us that we can do everything on our own, that we don't need God's help, but this is a lie. The sting of pride comes when we realize that we are not as self-sufficient as we thought, that our own efforts are not enough to bring us the peace and happiness we seek. Pride makes us strive for more—more success, more recognition, more power—but the more we chase after these things, the more we find ourselves empty and unfulfilled. This is the painful sting of pride: it promises so much but delivers so little. It leads us to believe that we can be satisfied through our own efforts, but in the end, it leaves us feeling more distant from God and from the true source of joy.

Pride also stings us by making it difficult to admit when we are wrong. Just as a scorpion strikes with its tail when it feels threatened, pride lashes out when we are confronted with our mistakes or failures. Instead of humbling ourselves and accepting correction, pride makes us defensive, unwilling to acknowledge our faults. This stubborn refusal to admit when we are wrong only deepens the sting of pride, because it prevents us from growing and learning from our mistakes. It isolates us from others, as people grow weary of dealing with someone who is always right and never willing to take responsibility for their actions. The sting of pride is not just felt in the immediate moment of conflict—it lingers, creating division and resentment in relationships. Over time, pride drives a wedge between us and the people we care about, because it prevents genuine connection and reconciliation. The more we allow pride to sting us, the more we push others away, leaving us isolated and alone.

The Bible warns us about the dangers of pride, and Revelation 9:10 uses the image of scorpions to illustrate how sin, including pride, has the power to hurt and destroy. Just as a scorpion's sting causes physical pain, pride causes emotional and spiritual pain, not only for the person who holds onto it but also for those around them. Pride makes us self-centered, causing us to act in ways that are harmful to others. It leads to jealousy, competition, and a lack of empathy, as we become more concerned with protecting our own image than with loving and serving others. Pride's sting is sharp because it turns us inward, focusing our attention on ourselves and blinding us to the needs and feelings of those around us. This kind of pride is destructive in relationships, as it creates an atmosphere of tension, competition, and resentment. Instead of building others up, pride causes us to tear others down in order to elevate ourselves.

One of the most painful aspects of pride's sting is the way it distances us from God. Pride makes us believe that we can do everything on our own, that we don't need God's help or guidance. It leads us to rely on our own strength and wisdom, rather than trusting in God's plan for our lives. This self-reliance is a form of spiritual pride, and it separates us from the grace and wisdom that God offers. The sting of pride comes when we realize that our own efforts are not enough, that we cannot find true peace or fulfillment apart from God. But by the time we come to this realization, the damage has often been done. We have distanced ourselves from God, made decisions that have led us away from His will, and hurt others in the process. The sting of pride is sharp because it leads us down a path of self-destruction, where we are cut off from the very source of life and love that we need most.

Pride also stings us by keeping us from repentance. Just as a scorpion's sting can cause paralysis, pride paralyzes our ability to seek forgiveness and healing. When we are full of pride, we don't want to admit that we need to repent. We don't want to acknowledge that we have sinned or that we have hurt others. Pride tells us that admitting our faults would make us look weak, that seeking forgiveness would mean giving up control. But the truth is, repentance is the path to healing and restoration. The longer we hold onto pride, the more we allow its sting to poison our hearts, keeping us from the freedom and peace that come from confessing our sins and receiving God's forgiveness. The Bible teaches us that God resists the proud but gives grace to the humble (James 4:6). When we humble ourselves and repent, we remove the sting of pride and open our hearts to the healing power of God's grace.

Pride's sting is not just a one-time event; it can continue to hurt us long after the initial wound. Just as a scorpion's venom can cause lasting pain, the consequences of pride can linger for months, years, or even a lifetime. Broken relationships, missed opportunities, and spiritual emptiness are some of the long-term effects of pride's sting. The pain caused by pride doesn't go away easily—it takes time, humility, and God's grace to heal the wounds that pride creates. But if we continue to hold onto pride, refusing to seek healing or change, the sting only deepens, causing more pain and more damage over time.

In order to avoid the sting of pride, we must choose humility. Humility is the antidote to pride's venom. It allows us to see ourselves and others through God's eyes, recognizing that we are all sinners in need of grace. Humility keeps us from relying on our own strength and wisdom, and instead, it leads us to trust in God's plan for our lives. It allows us to admit when we are wrong, to seek forgiveness when we have hurt others, and to rely on God's guidance in all things. Humility protects us from the sting of pride by keeping us grounded in the truth—that we are not self-sufficient, that we need God's help, and that we are called to love and serve others rather than elevate ourselves.

The Bible encourages us to walk in humility, following the example of Jesus, who, though He was God, humbled Himself and became a servant, even to the point of death on the cross (Philippians 2:5-8). Jesus showed us that true greatness comes not from prideful ambition but from humble service. When we choose humility, we protect ourselves from the sting of pride and open our hearts to the peace, joy, and fulfillment that come from living in God's will. Humility allows us to build strong, loving relationships with others, free from the tension and competition that pride creates. It also allows us to walk closely with God, trusting in His guidance and relying on His grace to lead us through life's challenges.

In conclusion, pride stings like a scorpion, causing sharp and painful consequences both for oneself and for others. Its sting is felt in the damage it causes to relationships, in the spiritual emptiness it creates, and in the way it distances us from God. Like the scorpions described in Revelation 9:10, pride has the power to hurt us deeply and to cause lasting pain. But we can avoid the sting of pride by choosing humility, by recognizing our need for God's guidance and grace, and by seeking to love and serve others rather than elevate ourselves. When we walk in humility, we protect ourselves from the venom of pride and open our hearts to the healing power of God's love and grace. Pride may sting sharply, but humility brings the peace and joy that pride can never offer. Let us choose humility, follow the example of Christ, and walk in the freedom and fulfillment that come from living according to God's will.

Conclusion

As we reach the conclusion of "The Animal of Pride," it's clear that pride is a force that Christians must constantly guard against, like a dangerous animal lurking in the shadows of our hearts. Pride is deceptive, sneaky, and relentless, always trying to find new ways to creep into our thoughts and actions. It may take the form of arrogance, self-righteousness, or even subtle comparisons to others, making us feel superior or more deserving. But no matter how it appears, pride always has the same effect—it separates us from God and distorts our relationships with others. Like a lion stalking its prey or a serpent slithering through the grass, pride is always waiting for an opportunity to take control of our lives. As Christians, we must remain vigilant, knowing that pride can rise up at any time, even in moments when we feel the most spiritual or strong. The battle against pride is not a one-time fight; it's an ongoing journey that requires humility, self-awareness, and dependence on God.

To continue in this journey, we must first recognize that humility is not a weakness—it's a strength. The world often tells us that we need to be bold, assertive, and confident in ourselves to succeed, but God's way is different. He calls us to be humble, to recognize our need for Him, and to rely on His strength rather than our own. Philippians 2:3 reminds us, "Let nothing be done through strife or vainglory; but in lowliness of mind let each esteem other better than themselves." This is the mindset we must adopt if we want to continue taming the animal of pride. It means putting others before ourselves, seeking to serve rather than to be served, and giving God the glory for every success, big or small. Humility is not about thinking less of ourselves, but about thinking of ourselves less. It's about making room for God to work through us, rather than trying to do everything on our own.

The next step in continuing this journey is to stay close to God through prayer and the study of His Word. Pride often takes root when we drift away from God, relying on our own wisdom and strength rather than seeking His guidance. But when we are intentional about spending time with God, we keep our hearts in the right place. Through prayer, we can ask God to reveal any hidden pride in our lives, to help us see ourselves as He sees us, and to give us the grace to walk in humility. His Word is full of wisdom on how to combat pride, and by reading and meditating on Scripture, we equip ourselves with the truth that helps us recognize and resist pride's subtle attacks. James 4:6 says, "But he giveth more grace. Wherefore he saith, God resisteth the proud, but giveth grace unto the humble." This verse is a powerful reminder that God's grace flows to those who humble themselves before Him, and it's a promise that He will help us in our fight against pride.

In our relationships, we must be intentional about practicing humility and love. Pride often shows itself in how we treat others—when we are impatient, unkind, or judgmental, it's usually because pride is at work in our hearts. But as followers of Christ, we are called to reflect His love and grace in our interactions with others. This means choosing forgiveness over resentment, understanding over judgment, and kindness over harshness. It means being willing to admit when we are wrong and seeking reconciliation when pride has caused division. Ephesians 4:2 states "With all lowliness and meekness, with longsuffering, forbearing one another in love;" By choosing to walk in humility, we can build stronger, more loving relationships that honor God and reflect His love to the world.

Another important aspect of continuing the fight against pride is to surround ourselves with a community of believers who will encourage us, hold us accountable, and help us grow in our faith. Pride often thrives in isolation, where there's no one to challenge our thinking or point out when we've gone astray. But when we are in community, we have the opportunity to learn from others, to hear different perspectives, and to be reminded of the importance of humility. Proverbs 27:17 says, "Iron sharpeneth iron; so a man sharpeneth the countenance of his friend." By staying connected to a community of believers, we create a support system that helps keep pride in check and encourages us to grow in humility.

Finally, the key to continuing in this journey is to keep our eyes on Jesus. He is the ultimate example of humility, and by following His lead, we can learn what it means to live a life free from the grip of pride. Philippians 2:5-8 describes how Jesus, though He was God, humbled Himself by becoming a servant and being obedient to the point of death on a cross. His life was a perfect demonstration of what it means to put others before yourself and to seek God's will above all else. As we strive to follow Jesus' example, we are reminded that true greatness comes not from exalting ourselves, but from humbling ourselves before God and others.

In conclusion, taming the animal of pride is a lifelong journey that requires constant vigilance, humility, and reliance on God. Pride is always lurking, ready to strike when we least expect it, but through God's grace, we can overcome it. By staying close to God in prayer, immersing ourselves in His Word, practicing humility in our relationships, surrounding ourselves with a community of believers, and keeping our eyes on Jesus, we can continue to walk the path of humility. It won't always be easy, and there will be moments when pride rears its ugly head, but with God's help, we can tame the animal of pride and live lives that reflect His love, grace, and humility. Let us go forward with hearts surrendered to God, trusting in His strength to keep us humble and free from the destructive power of pride.

Don't miss out!

Visit the website below and you can sign up to receive emails whenever Joshua Rhoades publishes a new book. There's no charge and no obligation.

https://books2read.com/r/B-A-AJLBB-YCFDF

BOOKS2READ

Connecting independent readers to independent writers.

Did you love *The Animal Of Pride*? Then you should read *Anchored In Truth Exploring The Depths of Psalm 119*[1] by Joshua Rhoades!

[2]

"Anchored in Truth: Exploring the Depths of Psalm 119" is an invitation to dive into one of the Bible's most profound passages, offering a deep exploration of faith, devotion, and the transformative power of God's Word. As the longest chapter in the Bible, Psalm 119 is a masterpiece of spiritual expression, structured as an intricate acrostic with each section beginning with a letter of the Hebrew alphabet. This psalm is not just a collection of verses; it is a meditation on the beauty and necessity of God's law. Through its 176 verses, the psalmist reveals a fervent love for God's commandments, a deep dependence on His guidance, and an unyielding pursuit of understanding and wisdom found only in the Scriptures.

"Anchored in Truth" invites you to explore the rich themes of Psalm 119, offering insights into how God's Word can shape, guide, and sustain a life of faith. This book is crafted not just to help you understand the words of this ancient psalm but to experience them in a way that profoundly impacts your daily walk with God. As you journey through each section, you will see how the psalmist's experiences resonate with the challenges and triumphs of your own spiritual life—whether it's seeking deliverance in trials, finding delight in God's statutes, or pleading for divine guidance.

---

1. https://books2read.com/u/mvPayX

2. https://books2read.com/u/mvPayX

This book is more than an intellectual study; it is a call to transformation. Psalm 119 urges us to anchor our lives in the unchanging truth of God's Word, making it the foundation of our character, decisions, and ultimate hope. The psalmist's devotion to God's law reminds us that Scripture is not just a set of rules or a historical text; it is the living Word of God, active and relevant in every aspect of our lives.

"Anchored in Truth" aims to inspire you to cultivate a deeper love for God's Word, seek His guidance in all things, and live out the truths found in these verses. As you read, may you be encouraged to stand firm in the faith, anchored in the unshakable truths of God's Word, and experience the wisdom, peace, and joy that come from living in alignment with His eternal commands.